PEOPLE IN MY Community

Veterinarians

Jared Siemens

LET'S READ
AV2 BY WEIGL
ADDED VALUE · AUDIO VISUAL

www.av2books.com

AV² provides enriched content that supplements and complements this book. Weigl's AV² books strive to create inspired learning and engage young minds in a total learning experience.

Your AV² Media Enhanced books come alive with...

Audio
Listen to sections of the book read aloud.

Key Words
Study vocabulary, and complete a matching word activity.

Video
Watch informative video clips.

Quizzes
Test your knowledge.

Embedded Weblinks
Gain additional information for research.

Slide Show
View images and captions, and prepare a presentation.

Try This!
Complete activities and hands-on experiments.

... and much, much more!

Go to **www.av2books.com**, and enter this book's unique code.

BOOK CODE

Y782688

AV² by Weigl brings you media enhanced books that support active learning.

Published by AV² by Weigl
350 5ᵗʰ Avenue, 59ᵗʰ Floor New York, NY 10118
Websites: www.av2books.com   www.weigl.com

Library of Congress Cataloging-in-Publication Data

Siemens, Jared.
 Veterinarians / Jared Siemens.
    pages cm. -- (People in my community)
 Includes index.
 ISBN 978-1-4896-3661-4 (hard cover : alk. paper) -- ISBN 978-1-4896-3662-1 (soft cover : alk. paper)
 ISBN 978-1-4896-3663-8 (single user ebk.) -- ISBN 978-1-4896-3664-5 (multi-user ebk.)
 1. Veterinarians--Juvenile literature. I. Title.
 SF756.S54 2016
 636.089092--dc23

                                    2015002873

Printed in the United States of America in Brainerd, Minnesota
1 2 3 4 5 6 7 8 9 0 19 18 17 16 15

022015
WEP270215

Project Coordinator: Jared Siemens
Design: Mandy Christiansen

Veterinarians

CONTENTS

People who live close together are part of a community.

The veterinarian is a person in my community.

A veterinarian works in an animal hospital.

An animal hospital is a place sick animals go to get healthy.

A veterinarian is an animal doctor.

She finds out why my pet is sick. She helps my pet to stay healthy.

I take my pet to a veterinarian for checkups.

He looks at my pet's ears, eyes, mouth, and nose.

11

The veterinarian looks at pictures made by a special camera.

These pictures help him see what is wrong.

The veterinarian puts a cast on my pet's leg when it is broken.

A cast helps keep the bone straight as it grows together again.

The veterinarian knows what medicine my pet needs to get well.

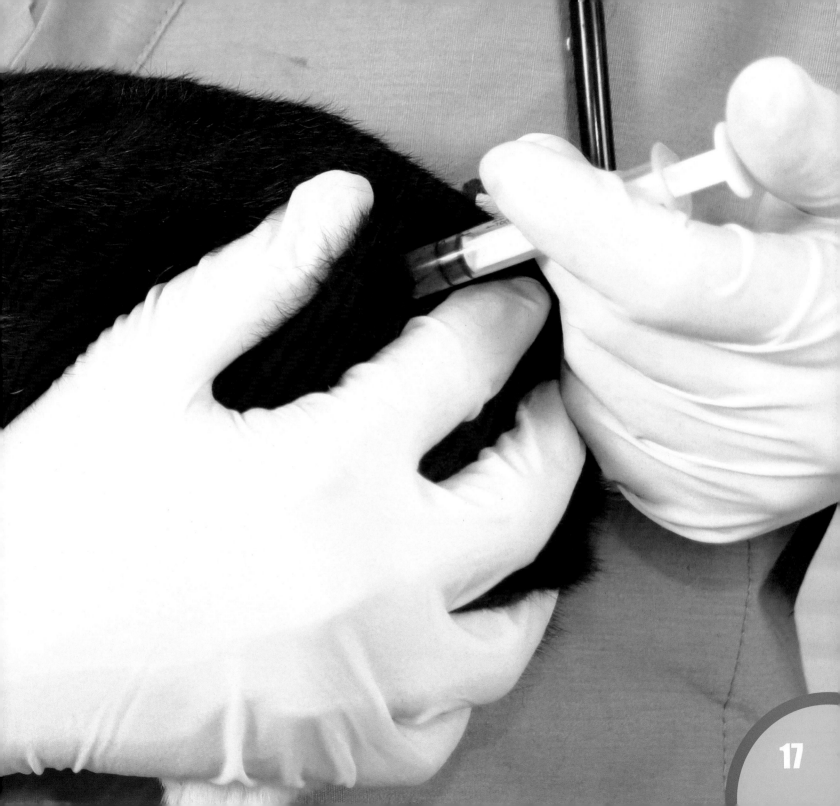

Veterinarians work on all kinds of animals.

18

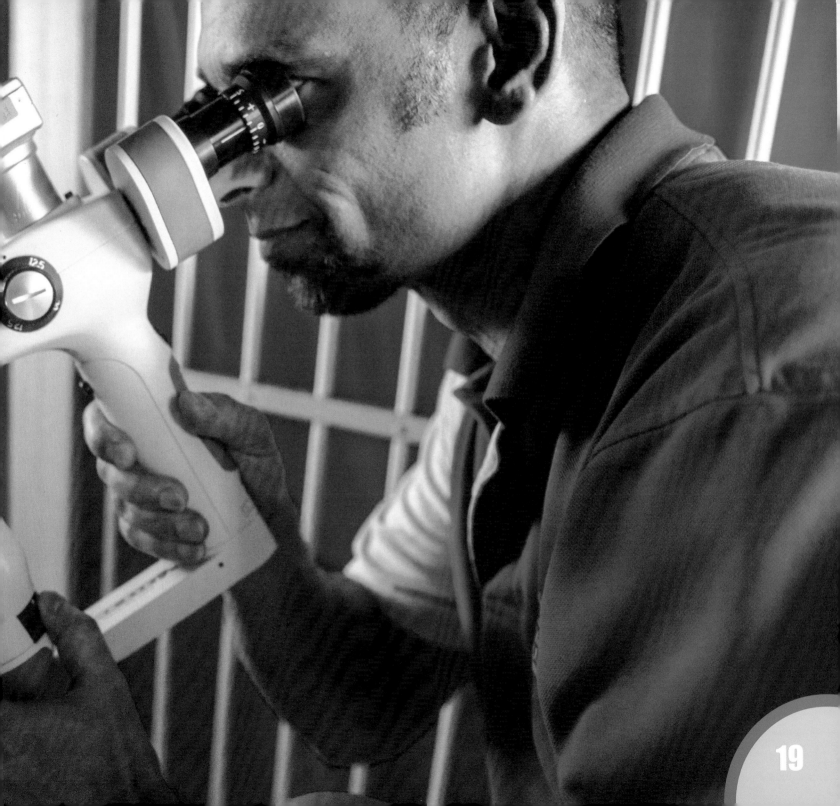

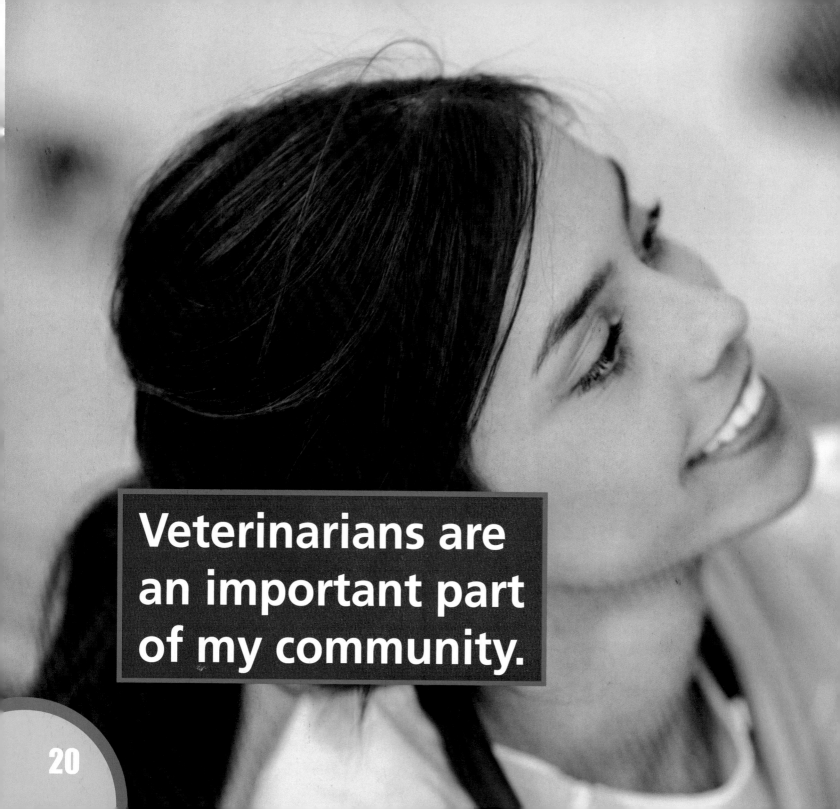

Veterinarians are an important part of my community.

See what you have learned about the veterinarian.

Describe what you see in each of the pictures.

KEY WORDS

Research has shown that as much as 65 percent of all written material published in English is made up of 300 words. These 300 words cannot be taught using pictures or learned by sounding them out. They must be recognized by sight. This book contains 54 common sight words to help young readers improve their reading fluency and comprehension. This book also teaches young readers several important content words, such as proper nouns. These words are paired with pictures to aid in learning and improve understanding.

Page	Sight Words First Appearance
4	a, are, close, live, of, part, people, together, who
5	in, is, my, the
6	an, animal, works
7	get, go, place, to
9	finds, helps, out, she, why
10	for, I, take
11	and, at, eyes, he, looks
12	by, made, pictures
13	him, see, these, what
14	it, on, puts, when
15	again, as, grows, keep
16	knows, needs, well
18	all, kinds
20	important

Page	Content Words First Appearance
4	community
5	person, veterinarian
6	animal hospital
8	animal doctor
9	pet
10	checkups
11	ears, mouth, nose
12	camera
14	cast, leg
15	bone
16	medicine

Check out www.av2books.com for activities, videos, audio clips, and more!

1. Go to www.av2books.com.
2. Enter book code. **Y782688**
3. Fuel your imagination online!

www.av2books.com